Localizing NGO Leadership in Lao Civil Society

Takehiro Ono

北樹出版

Takehiro Ono,

Localizing NGO Leadership in Lao Civil Society,

2021.9.30

ISBN978-4-7793-0669-3

ⓒ2021, Takehiro Ono, printed in Japan

This edition is published by Hokuju Shuppan Co.Ltd.,

Nakameguro1-2-6 Meguro-ku Tokyo-to Japan,

Tel. ＋81-3-3715-1525

URL：http://www.hokuju.jp

PREFACE

It has been nearly 20 years since I conducted this research in 2002 about the Lao People's Democratic Republic (hereafter Lao PDR). Lao PDR was established in 1975 and while supported by socialist policies and has achieved impressive economic growths during recent decades. However, these growths seem to be relatively slow in terms of its civil society. To manage and control the people's organizations, the Decree on Associations was enacted in 2009 (replaced in 2017) and the Decree on International Non-Governmental Organizations (INGOs) was enacted in 2010. This research aimed to find some ways to make more space in Lao civil society by facilitating organizational development in the previous generation. I believe that some people in NGO communities would draw important lessons to their current practices on organizational development and human resource management from the past experiences.

The original purpose of the research was to determine the most important capacity building component for the localization process, focusing on international NGOs in Lao PDR. Data was collected from Lao senior staff and expatriate NGO representatives (over 20 informants in total) by face-to-face interviews during June-July 2002, in Vientiane Capital. Each interview was focused on 1) perception of localization, 2) organizational capacity, 3) vision of localization, 4) NGO leadership, and 5) local NGOs applying the organizational capacity building model by the IDRC (International Development Research Centre). Informants showed a positive understanding to a definition of localization: as a process of organizational change focusing on how to delegate organizational performance initiatives from the international side (expatriates) to the local side (local staff). Furthermore, they assessed currently their "human resource management" and "program management" as most advanced delegated areas. Through the data analysis and lessons from existing Lao leaders in international NGOs, I concluded that "strategic leadership" was the most important capacity building component towards localization which is one of the possible ways to enlarge a civil society in Lao PDR. Since many NGOs served various levels in the education sector and/or applied educational methods in the other sectors as well, the development of leadership capacity could contribute not only to their NGO management but also to the wide range of education in Lao civil society.

This publication is a summary of my research activities including the essence of my master thesis submitted to School for International Training (SIT), Brattleboro, Vermont, USA in 2004. I would like to acknowledge the continuous consultation given by Prof. Paul G. Ventura, SIT and the precious data from the many informants from the NGO community in the various sectors. Without their sincere contributions, this research could not be done. Finally, my previous organization where I served for more than 20 years, Shanti Volunteer Association supported me fully both before and after this research. I learned from the executive members and staff in both headquarters in Tokyo and overseas field offices, and of course, Lao local staff gave me a lot of insights during my stay in Lao PDR. It is my wish that this publication is still informative for those who wish to progress civil society in the world.

Takehiro Ono
Hokkaido, Japan

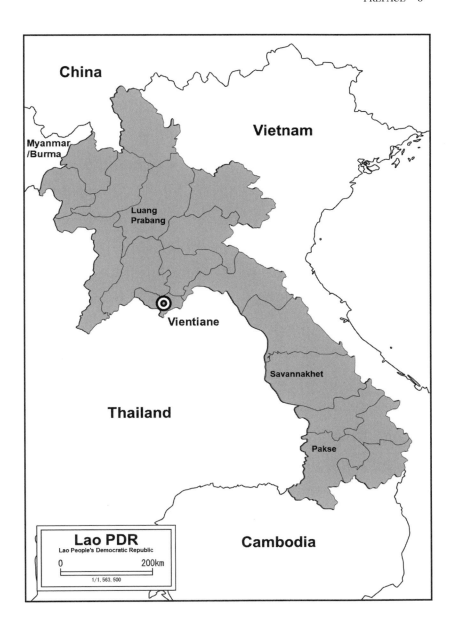

China

Vietnam

Myanmar /Burma

Luang Prabang

Vientiane

Savannakhet

Thailand

Pakse

Cambodia

Lao PDR
Lao People's Democratic Republic

0   200km

1/1, 563, 500

CONTENTS

Localizing NGO Leadership in Lao Civil Society

INTRODUCTION

1. My Experience in Lao PDR

Lao PDR is a small mountainous, landlocked country in Southeast Asia, surrounded by five countries: China, Myanmar, Thailand, Cambodia, and Vietnam. Because of its geographical setting and historical factors, there are five million people consisting of forty-five ethnic groups with different linguistic and cultural backgrounds. The population is divided for political and administrative reasons into three major categories called Lao Loum (Lowland dwellers forming 60% of the total population); Lao Tueng (Midland or Slope dwellers forming 30% of the total population); and Lao Soung (Highland dwellers forming 10% of the total population). Since most people heavily depend on subsistence agriculture, the government's primary development is agricultural-based national construction. Two-thirds of the 238,000 sq km of the country are mountainous areas inhabited by minority groups, the Lao Tueng and Lao Soung. Many of them are still struggling to find basic human needs in their communities. This is one of reasons why multilateral, bilateral, and private non-governmental organizations (NGOs) have various development projects targeting those people.

I worked for two Japanese NGOs in Lao PDR for a total of ten years (1991–2002). For the first two years, I was in charge of administration and accounting at *Japan International Volunteer Center (JVC)* and I supported several "Women In Development" (WID) projects. Later, I transferred to the *Shanti Volunteer Association (SVA)*, another Japanese NGO, to work as educational project coordinator, acting-director, and director. During my stay in Lao PDR, I observed and experienced multiple dimensions of development or growth at both micro and macro levels. In particular, the managerial experience I gained in the last several years has brought me a lot of ideas and experience for organizational capacity building. One of my major issues was how to develop an effective process for shifting management leadership from Japanese expatriates to Lao staff, becoming a Lao-directed organization. This situation, where foreign expatriates are predominantly employed to manage development projects, is not unique to Japanese programs. Other organizations experience the same issues.

2. NGOs in Lao PDR

According to the Directory of NGOs in Lao PDR 2000, there are 56 international NGOs in Lao PDR. Some of them started development operations in 1973, such as Quaker Service Lao PDR or the American Friend Service Committee. The following list of the international NGOs seems to reflect the historical international relations of Lao PDR (Table 1). The percentages of NGOs working in different sectors are: human resources development (31%); health (22%); education (11%); data collection and analysis (11%); emergency and humanitarian relief (7%); agriculture; forestry and fisheries (7%); social development (7%); and natural resources (4%) (Directory of NGOs in Lao PDR 2000, p 142).

The term NGO refers to foreign-based, non-profit development organizations since Lao NGOs do not exist. Because the government of Lao PDR has not provided legislation to obtain the legal status to those private voluntary associations by Lao nationals, the groups or the movements are usually registered as private schools, companies, or a project of UN organizations or other international NGOs. People are not allowed to start associations and/or activities without the legal status or approval by the authorities. Issues like people's rights such as freedom of association and speech are still limited in this country, and the government would probably have its own economic and social reasons for seeking to limit expansion of the development cooperation program beyond existing NGO boundaries. Motivated individuals and groups may hesitate to submit request letters for getting approval for private NGOs and they

Table 1. International NGOs in Lao PDR

	Name of INGOs		Name of INGOs
1	Action contre la Faim (ACF)	29	International Federation of Red Cross and Red Crescent Societies (IFRC)
2	Action Nord Sud (ANS)	30	International Volunteers Association of Japan (IV-Japan)
3	Adventist Development and Relief Agency (ADRA)	31	Japan International Volunteer Center (JVC)
4	Association for Sending Picture Books (ASPB)	32	Shanti Volunteer Association (SVA)
5	Association Medicale Franco-Asiatique (AMFA)	33	Lao Mission Center (LMC)
6	Australian Red Cross (ARC)	34	Medicins Sans Frontieres (MSF)
7	Australian Volunteers International (AIV)	35	Mennonite Central Committee (MCC)
8	Canadian Volunteer Organisation (CUSO)	36	Mines Advisory Group (MAG)
9	CARE International (CARE)	37	Minsai Center
10	Church World Service (CWS)	38	Netherlands Red Cross (NRC)
11	Comite de Cooperation avec le Lao PDR (CCL)	39	Norwegian Church Aid (NCA)
12	Community Aid Abroad (CAA)	40	Norwegian People's Aid (NPA)
13	Concern Worldwide (CONCERN)	41	Oxfam Solidarity Belgium (Oxfam)
14	Consortium	42	Pact
15	Cooperation and Development (CESVI)	43	Quaker Service Laos (QSL)
16	Cooperation Internationale pour le Development et la Solidarite (CIDSE)	44	Redd Barna (RB)
17	Cooperative Orthotic and Prosthetic Enterprise (COPE)	45	Save the Children Australia (SCA)
18	Damien Foundation Belgium (DFB)	46	Save the Children UK (SCF-UK)
19	Danish Red Cross (DRC)	47	Service Fraternel d'Entraide (SFE)
20	Deutsche Welthungerhilfe/German Agro Action (DWHH/GAA)	48	Swiss Red Cross (SRC)
21	Ecoles Sans Frontieres (ESF)	49	The Leprosy Mission International (TLMI)
22	Enfants et Developpement (EED)	50	Voluntary Services Overseas (VSO)
23	Family Planning Australia (FPA)	51	Wildlife Conservation Society (WCS)
24	Food for the Hungry International (FHI)	52	World Concern (WC)
25	Green Life Association (GL)	53	Global Association of People's Education (GAPE)
26	Handicap International (HI)	54	World University Service Canada (WUSC)
27	Health Frontiers (HF)	55	World Vision (WV)
28	Health Unlimited (HU)	56	ZOA

Source: reprinted and modified with a list of *"Directory of NGOs in Lao PDR 2000"*.

seek the way to become private schools, companies, or projects of international organizations. Thus, the means to becoming a local NGO are very much limited in Lao
society, and consequently there are very few organizations authorized and capable of
taking on the responsibilities currently conducted by international NGOs. Therefore, my research is focused on another pattern of Lao-directed NGOs, or localized
international NGOs.

There are at least four international NGOs, which can provide examples of the
Lao-directed NGOs. These are: Community Aid Abroad (CAA, or Oxfam Australia);
Cooperation Internationale pour le Development et la Solidarite (CIDSE); Minsai
Center; and Association for Sending Picture Books (ASPB). CAA, CIDSE, ASPB
shifted their managers to Lao nationals from foreign expatriates in the middle of
1990. Minsai Center had a Lao manager since the beginning of their operations in
1996. Minsai Center has a policy of not sending foreign residential managers to the
field office. Except for temporary advisory expatriates or consultants, the above four
offices are completely managed by indigenous Lao directors. Using Lao as the major
working language, the environment seems much more autonomous than in the other
international NGOs. The existence of these pioneer NGOs was the trigger for my research subject. I assume that they have advanced experience and information that
can contribute to the achievement of a successful localization process in Lao PDR.

3.   Lao-Directed Organizations

"Lao-directed organizations" will be used to describe as organizations led or managed
by experienced Lao senior staff. There are basically two emerging patterns: One is
the case that international NGOs would shift organizational management from foreign expatriates to Lao staff after a period of capacity building. I would like to call it
localization in this paper. The second step towards more effective development strategies could be achieved by establishing "indigenous NGOs" directed by motivated
and qualified Lao individuals or groups. However, repeatedly, the establishment of

Lao NGOs is very difficult. Some Lao groups have submitted proposals to establish NGOs, but the government has rejected them for some reasons. Since there are very few examples of the latter, I focus on the former case, the localization process of international NGOs and organizational capacity building.

4. Organizational Capacity Building

Localization within international NGOs is seen as a process of organizational capacity building, emphasizing self-management by Lao staff. I assume that leadership capacity may be one of the most critical factors in this organizational development process because fostering leadership is deeply based on personal characteristics and trustful working experience. In this paper, I will analyze various existing levels of localization in Lao PDR, compared with some examples in other developing countries. Furthermore, to create highly effective, indigenous organizations and even to commence the process of indigenous NGOs in building a Lao civil society, I would like to propose an appropriate model to bring about successful localization.

In organizing my research, I identified my major research question and several related ones:

5. Research Questions and Rationale

- What is the most important capacity building component of the process of localizing an International NGO in Lao PDR?

To support the above research question, I will address the following related questions:

- What is localization? Which dimensions should be considered in organizational capacity building towards localization?

- Why do international NGOs localize? Why would they not localize?
- What is the role of leadership in the process of localization?
- What are the unique characteristics of International NGOs operating development projects in Lao PDR?
- What are the lessons from International NGOs, which already have Lao directors?
- What factors in the current political situation would help or hinder in establishing 'Indigenous NGOs' in Lao PDR?

Lao PDR, to date, has not shown a very positive attitude to approving or promoting indigenous NGOs, enlarging civil society, and allowing local organizations to take initiatives for grassroots development in the country. This situation might not last longer because a more transparent administrative movement (such as Doi Moi in Vietnam) has progressively been introduced in the neighboring socialist countries with which Lao PDR has close political relations. To facilitate this movement in this country, international NGOs could develop Lao social leaders, who understand people's power and organizations, and have capacity to create Local NGOs which are essentially independent from both Lao government and international organizations.

As an international NGO worker who has worked in Lao PDR, I would like to contribute what I have learned into people in this country, particularly senior Lao workers to increase their initiatives in this society. They have been coordinating development activities among their governmental counterparts, expatriate supervisors, and beneficiaries under various political pressures. Some of them are struggling with this process, and others are waiting for the 'right moment' to take more initiative in managing development activities in their country with their own language and decision-making style. This process must be perceived by the Lao government as a collective effort at improving the development of the country, rather than as a political threat to social security. I hope this research on localization will suggest important steps in developing local NGOs and expanding civil society in Lao PDR.

LITERATURE REVIEW

1. Localization

1.1 Definition of Localization

"Localization" is often used to refer to the de-centralization of state power or multinational cooperation. However, in this paper, I define localization as a process of organizational change focusing on how to delegate organizational performance initiatives from the international side (expatriates) to the local side (local staff). To describe "localized" entities in Lao PDR, I will use the term 'Lao-directed NGOs', which means NGOs led by Lao mangers, not by expatriates sent by the NGO's headquarters. Organizational structure, communication systems, leadership, human resources (HR) or financial management are also important issues. In this paper, I focus on leadership aspects because, like states and international organizations, leadership is at the heart or the engine of development NGOs.

1.2 Two categories of Lao-Directed NGOs

The first category of Lao-Directed NGOs is 'indigenous or local NGOs', which are led by Lao leaders since their establishment. As I mentioned in my introduction, in Lao PDR all NGOs are international NGOs because the government, for political reasons, has not yet legally approved establishment of NGOs. A study of Asian Development Bank (ADB) summarized that "the Government does not consider setting up local NGOs a priority, since mass organizations are in place from central to village level, and these can motivate and encourage the participation of villagers for the development of the country" (ADB, 1999). The NGOs decree and guidelines are provided only for international NGOs not local NGOs (Government of Lao PDR, 1998). There are several Lao voluntary associations, which requested for an official status but were rejected probably due to lack of valid legislation. Some development associations thus decided to register as business investors or as private schools.

Second, localization, or international NGOs making a positive change by appointing local development partners, is an alternative method to increase NGO participation in the civil sector. There are many similar terms to describe this situation such as decentralization, 'indigenization', self-management, evolution, devolution, and nationalization. In this context, I would use the term 'localization' for the process whereby local organizations gradually take more responsibility for development activities.

In addition, local NGOs could be created after international NGOs are fully localized in some organizational development processes. In other words, creating local NGOs could be a final goal of the localization process because it can be a continuous process (see table 2). Some local NGOs can also become international NGOs in other countries. For example, BRAC, the largest Bangladeshi NGO has recently started to operate rehabilitation and development projects in Afghanistan.

1.3   Changing Roles of NGOs in the Developed Countries

These days, NGOs in developed countries have been very active and powerful in enlarging civil society. Some of them have established affiliates in other countries to extend their helping hands, for example, Grameen Bank in Bangladesh and ALOP in Latin America (Lindenberg and Bryant, 2001). Therefore, NGOs in developed countries, which have been working for development in the developing countries, face a shift in their major focus areas on back-up support rather than field operations.

David Korten describes four generations of NGOs in his excellent book, *"Getting to the 21ˢᵗ Century: Voluntary Action and the Global Agenda"*. He points out that roles of northern NGOs would change from relief/welfare (Generation One), small-scale, self-reliant local development (Generation Two), sustainable systems development (Generation Three) and people's movement (Generation Four) (Korten, 1989). He suggests that "international NGOs being told that if they are to have any legitimate function in development in the South, they must first transform themselves and seek new and more timely roles in developing the capabilities of indigenous NGOs and voluntary sectors" (Korten, 1989). Thus, the role of international NGOs in developing countries is changing into more indirect intervention along with the growth of indigenous NGOs. Movement towards localization is supported by these NGO development trends.

1.4   Central Units Versus Affiliates

In the context of international NGOs' involvement in developing countries, the localization process is crafting new power relations between South and North within the organizations. Furthermore, the relations can be duplicated in those between headquarters (North) and branch/field operation offices (South) in a single International NGO. In *Going Global,* Marc Lindenberg and Coralie Bryant describe "the classification was based on a continuum of differences in rights and responsibilities of central units versus affiliates." This is one of the results of a 1998 retreat with senior leaders of six well established NGOs: CARE, Oxfam, Medecins Sans Frontierers, PLAN International, World Vision International, and Save the Children. The leaders discussed common future challenges in development. The classification shows how each element of an organization maintains its autonomy compared with central units (see Table 2). The process of localizations is central to all of these concerns. The following table shows the breadth of views canvassed for elements of developmental NGOs.

Each item on the continuum describes a form of organizational autonomy. There are five categories such as *the Separate Independent Organization, the Weak Umbrella, the Confederation, the Federation,* and *the Unitary Corporate.* In the Separate Independent Organization model, the affiliates maintain decision-making authority from their

Table2. Views of Alternative Models for Associational Structures as Expressed at NGO Presidents' Retreat I: Bellagio

	Separate Independent Organizations & Coalitions	Weak Umbrella Coordinating Mechanisms	Confederations	Federations	Unitary Corporate
INTERNATIONAL RELIEF AND DEVELOPMENT NGO SERVICE PROVIDERS					
Locus of decision-making	Individual members	Individual members	Center has weak coordinating capacity with strong individual members	Center has strong authority over system-wide decisions than members	Central
Who sets global norms	No one	Individual members	Members with central coordination	Central headquarters and board	Central headquarters and board
Central enforcement mechanisms	None	Weak moral suasion	Moral suasion and limited sanctions like expulsion	Stronger sanctions like withholding	Strong central enforcement and incentive system
Resource acquisition methods	At member level	At member level	Primarily at member level but some common acquisition	Primarily at member level but some common acquisition	Centrally and globally acquired
Resource allocation methods	At member level	At member level	Largely member level with some central allocation	Largely member level with even more central allocation	Central allocation
Common systems	None	None	A few primary financial & programmatic quality	More common systems	Common systems
Common name	No	Yes	Yes	Yes	Yes
Common logo	No	Sometimes	Sometimes	Often	Often
Franchising	No	No	Sometimes	Sometimes	Yes

Source: Adapted from Young, Dennis R. *Local Autonomy in a Franchise Age: Structural Change in National Volunteer Associations. Nonprofit and Voluntary Sector Quarterly* 18, No.2 Summer 1989., 101-17.

international headquarters, backed up by their own strong board, fundraising, and programs. The Weak Umbrella model shows virtual autonomy but some coordination mechanisms to share necessary common information. In the Confederation model, strong members delegate some coordination, standard setting, and resource allocation duties to the central offices. However, actual decision-making is more participatory. In the Federated model, the center has strong powers for standard setting and resource acquisition but affiliates have separate boards and implementation capacity. Finally, in the Unitary model, there is only one global organization with a single board and central headquarters which makes resource acquisition, allocation, and program decisions at all levels. There are branch offices around the world, which are staffed by the central body and which implement centrally taken decisions around the world in their constituent bodies.

Although this classification is based on analysis of the six large well-known international relief and development NGOs, it may be applicable to other International NGOs to identify future directions in their organizational structures. Furthermore, they will also be good models to determine a goal of localization as an ideal relationship between the center and the periphery. Localization toward the Separated Independent Organizations model might bring about the desirable result of establishing local NGOs.

The other four models show different degrees of localization within a larger framework of international NGOs. Lindenberg and Bryant state that leaders of the six international NGOs believe the Independent Organizations with Weak Umbrella Coordination, Confederations, and Federations are dominant among the larger Northern relief and development organizations. Currently, they consider MSF in the Weak Umbrella, CARE International in the Confederations, and PLAN International in the Federations (Lindenberg and Bryant, 2001, p.143). These data indicate that some international NGOs in Lao PDR are already involved in the streams of the above three future organizational structures. It means that their localization goals and development strategies are not focused to establish independent local organizations but they tend to maintain the same norms, common names and logs, and central administrative mechanisms.

This model, vertical classification in particular, is useful in identifying degrees of localization for each International NGO. It provides an ideal localized formation for the future. I will apply this model to analyze the goals of localization in addition to the comments of informants of international NGOs in Lao PDR.

1.5 Examples of Localization

There must be many ways of moving towards localization in the NGO development fields around the world. However, most of them might be unpublished and kept as internal documents or as experiences among the staff members. I introduce four localization cases of US-based international NGOs to understand more about the reality of localization prior to the living cases in Lao PDR.

1.5.1 PACT Bangladesh to PRIP Trust

PACT, a-US based NGO which focuses on strengthening capacity of grassroots organizations, coalitions and networks, started a project in Bangladesh in the early 1990s. The executive director (American) and vice-director (Bangladeshi) of PACT Bangladesh worked together for a long time, and finally decided to form a local NGO, called PRIP Trust. The Vice-Director, Ms. Aroma Goon, became Executive Director with support from the former director. However, at the beginning of her leadership, she struggled in fundraising activities because USAID ceased its support. Fortunately, CIDA (Canadian International Development Agency) showed no hesitation in providing long-term funding. She was also busily engaged in trust building among NGOs and capacity building among staff. PRIP Trust was able to progress with the 'indigenization' process with active board members and highly motivated staff. She described this process as 'indigenization' instead of localization (Parameshwar, unknown).

This is not a true case of localizing an international NGO, but it can be more accurately identified as establishing a local NGO. I think this type of drastic organizational transition requires strong leadership like Ms. Aroma Goon. About PACT's position, Ms. Goon says, "PACT is a friend and partner today, not a conduit or funder." (Parameshwar, unknown). Considering the View of Alternative Models in Table 1, this case is an example of being in the Separate Independent Organizations and Coalitions stage.

1.5.2　A Project of World Learning to DEVCENTRE (Malawi)

The second example is a case from World Learning, which is also an US-based NGO. In 1990, jointly with USAID, World Learning started implementing a project called Services in Health, Agriculture, and Rural Enterprise Development (SHARED) in Malawi in Southeastern Africa. A purpose of this project, in fact, was to create a local NGO which deals with the SHARED project in Malawi. This is a very unique example of purposeful localization. It means that the localization was strategically planned to establish an independent indigenous organization. David Payton, Program Manager for World Learning, states positively in his article, "ten years of capacity building and five years of transforming SHARED has positioned the DevCentre as a leading local NGO service organization" (Payton, 2001). This case highlights the importance of designing the localization process since the beginning of international involvement, and illustrates the desirability of capacity building and a transition plan for a successful result.

1.5.3　CARE Thailand to CARE Thailand Foundation

CARE International consists of the 11 national members and 61 country offices around the world. CARE Thailand started its mission in 1979 in response to a massive influx of Cambodian refugees. Then, after a ten-year involvement in this tragedy, it shifted to development projects in response to Thai social and environmental problems. Major projects were focused on sustainable agricultural assistance for northern upland minorities and community-based HIV/AIDS education and prevention.

CARE USA, which is a supporter of CARE Thailand, considered the merits of "indige-nization" very seriously. The main reason for "indigenization" was the rapid econom-ic growth of Thailand and the difficulties associated with fundraising for projects. Lo-cal staff in Thailand were considered by headquarters to be very competent and deeply committed. In particular, Mr. Promboon Panitchpakdi, the Thai Program Di-rector (currently Country Representative of CARE Thailand Foundation) was per-ceived as "the guy who's going to lead this organization one day (Tarr, 1995)." In most discussions, CARE USA and Thailand used the term "indigenization" to de-scribe their efforts at localization. They also chose a broader and less value-laden term "organizational change."

From long discussions, including outside consultancy, the organization had five pos-sible options for CARE Thailand: "status quo", "minimizing the size", "phasing out en-tirely", "phasing out and setting up a Thai NGO", and "dual status." To create a win-win situation for both CARE USA and CARE Thailand, the organization chose the fifth option, "dual status as a Thai NGO and a CARE member". In 1995, the ad-vanced entity started as a Thai-registered local NGO, 'CARE Thailand Foundation' as well as one of CARE International's members. Mr. Promboon Panitchpakdi was ap-pointed to take leadership of the transitional enterprise.

1.5.4 Church World Service Cambodia (ongoing process)

Church World Service (CWS) is a relief, development, and refugee assistance organ-ization, which carries out development projects in over 80 countries. One of the pro-jects in Cambodia focuses on capacity development in indigenous NGOs and CBOs (Community Based Organizations). Furthermore, CWS Cambodia plans for the management and program support systems to be managed and administrated by Cambodian staff. For example, its strategic plan indicates how to decrease numbers and involvement of expatriates step-by-step.

CWS has designed and implemented a variety of training programs in both development techniques and management skills for people in Cambodian NGOs, CBOs, and CWS itself according to their own needs. Capacity building for own staff is also planned well and focused on self-management. A management vision of CWS is very clear in the following statement: "Our vision is that CWS Cambodia will be an organization managed and administrated primarily by Cambodians" (Church World Service Cambodia, 2001). Coordinators for projects are all Cambodians; however, the director has not yet shifted to local leadership. The reason can be simply stated that the current expatriates have not seen any strong and trustworthy leaders among Cambodian staff. There is no clue that they have a strategy or plan to recruit Cambodian directors instead of choosing from their own human resources.

2. Organizational Capacity Building

2.1 Areas of Organizational Capacity

As one of the significant issues in organizational development, the process of localization seems very difficult, but the results are important in making a positive impact on the NGO development paradigm. In this section, I would like to focus on organizational capacity building leading towards the objective of localization.

There are many ways to categorize dimensions of organizational capacity. For example, one organization assessment tool, DOSA (Discussion-Oriented Organizational Self-Assessment), uses six models: *human resource management, financial resource management, service delivery, external relations, organizational learning,* and *strategic management* (Levinger and Bloom, 1997). Another organizational auditing tool, EEMO (Elements of Effectively Managed Organization) categorizes organizational capacity into the following eight elements: *mission, planning, structure, people, systems, results & quality, leadership,* and *relationships* (Allison and Kaye, 1999). In this paper, I would like to use an outline by IDRC (International Development Research

Table 3.   Seven Areas of Organizational Capacity and Their Various Components

Area	Components
Strategic Leadership	Leadership, strategic planning, governance, structure, and niche management
Human Resources	Planning, staffing, developing, apprising and rewarding, and maintaining effective human-resource relations
Financial Management	Financial planning, financial accountability, and financial statements and systems
Infrastructure	Facilities management and technology management
Program Management	Planning, implementing, and monitoring programs and projects
Organizational Process	Problem-solving, decision-making, communications, and monitoring and evaluation
Institutional linkages	Planning, implementing, and monitoring networks and partnerships

Source: Lusthaus, Charles., Adrien, Marie-Helene., Anderson, Gary., and Carden, Fred.
   Enhancing Organizational Performance: A Toolbox For Self-Assessment. IDRC: International Development
   Research Centre, 1999. 62.

Centre) as a reference for the further discussion of localization (see Table 3). In comparison with DOSA and EEMO, each framework is over-lapped enough to capture a total picture of organizational capacity.

2.2   Training for Organizational Capacity Building

As I mentioned, localization can be considered as a process of organizational change focusing on how to delegate organizational performance initiatives from the international side (expatriates) to the local side (local staff). This is not a thing which will happen in one night or be formed naturally. As we saw in four different cases of localization, it is a long-term planned process with several series of capacity building objectives and considerable training resources. These exercises must be targeted at senior local staff and focused on both program and operational management capacities.

Repeatedly, one of my related research questions is to understand the role of leadership in the process of localization. I assumed that strategic leadership is one of the most important organizational capacities to lead a successful localization strategy. At the same time, it might be the most difficult capacity dimension to be nurtured and acquired. In the next section, I will discuss the uniqueness of leadership capacity which international NGOs would like to identify among their local senior staff.

3. NGO Leadership

3.1 What is NGO Leadership?

Unlike political or business leaders, NGO leaders are not under the same public scrutiny and have not been studied much yet. According to Alan Fowler (2000), recent leadership studies focusing on NGOs show a number of common weaknesses:

1) domination by North American and Anglo-Saxon conditions and experience;

2) distinctive features of leading non-profit organizations are weakly demonstrated; therefore, much of the analysis would equally apply to business;

3) leadership is seen as the function of a governing board;

4) this perspective does not commonly reflect the situation in the South and East of non-profit organizations as leader-centric organizations; and,

5) many writers pay attention to management, rather than leadership.

He describes a uniqueness of NGO leadership by quoting a statement by Peter Drucker: "the successful leader of a non-profit organization embodies the organization's mission - personal resonance with followers is critical for organizations that rely on motivations that are not principally informed by competition and money (business) or conformity and power (government)". It seems obvious that NGO leaders or civic leaders are very different from business and political leaders.

After several discussions to challenge the above common weaknesses of studies of NGO leadership, Alan Fowler concludes; "exemplary NGDO (Non-Governmental Development Organization) leaders are both creative artists and competent artisans. Artistry equates with inspiration to see society work in a different way and to communicate this vision to others so that they are motivated to act. Artisanship requires the skill to create an organization through which those motivated to act can do so effectively and honestly, and once created if requires skill to remain respected and viable to be insightful and agile" (Fowler, 2000, p. 174).

The question is, in the localization process, whether International NGOs would foresee the appearance of the above-described leaders in their future organizational status. If yes, their final goal of localization might be focused on creating separated independent organizations (Lindenberg and Bryant, 2001, p. 141) with full autonomy from central units, according to the classification shown in Table 2. Only in truly independent organizations could the new Lao leaders implement their own development vision without intervention by the mother organizations, government agencies, or bureaucrats. In that case, they are already beyond status of "localized" International NGOs, and may be called "local" or "indigenous" NGOs.

3.2 NGO Leadership Development and Localization

Making decisions is one of the most important functions performed by leaders in planning and implementing programs, solving internal problems, selecting appropriate staff, setting job assignments, spending budgets, and so on. Furthermore, in the case of NGO leaders, 'making decisions' is usually shared with others; therefore, the style is also called collective leadership or participative leadership (Smille, 2001, p. 147). Most theorists would acknowledge the following four decision procedures as distinct and meaningful:

1) **Autocratic Decision**: The manager makes a decision alone without asking for the opinions or suggestions of other people, and these people

have no direct influence on the decision; there is no participation.

2) **Consultation**: The manager asks other people for their ideas and opinions, then makes a decision alone after seriously considering their suggestions and concerns.

3) **Joint Decision**: The manager meets with others to discuss the decision problem and they make a decision together; the manager has no more influence over the final decision than any other participant.

4) **Delegation**: The manager gives an individual or a group the authority and responsibility for making a decision; the manager usually specifies limits within which the final choice must fall, and prior approval may or may not be required before the decision can be implemented (Yukl, 1998, p. 123).

In the beginning of this paper, I defined localization as a process of delegation in organizational performance initiatives. The idea may be broken down to the individual performance level. The critical part of localization depends on how successfully expatriates in managerial roles can delegate multiple decisions of daily work and visionary direction to Lao senior staff as the next leaders. In other words, localization can be described, in part, as a process of leadership development and delegation.

3.3 Development of Leadership Skills

According to Gary Yukl, there are three approaches for developing leadership skills: leadership training programs, developmental activities, and self-development activities. Formal training programs are widely used to improve leadership in organizations. Some larger organizations may conduct training programs by themselves, but use tailor-made workshops implemented by consulting companies, institutes, and universities. Development activities include practical techniques along with operational job assignments. They take such forms as coaching, mentoring, special assignments with current jobs, special assignments on temporary leave from the current job, and a promotion or transfer that provides new challenges and opportunities for skill development. Self-development activities consist of reading books, viewing videos, listening to audiotapes, and using interactive computer programs, all carried out by individuals (Yukl, 1998).

In the context of NGO leadership, Alan Fowler highlights the relationship between training programs and development activities: "in the short term, fostering succession calls for less reliance on training and more on extended process that give structured reflection on experience allied to mentoring and personal guidance." The reliability of this statement will be one significant issue to look at for each existing international NGO. Furthermore, to nurture NGO leaders in the long term, he suggests we should "get young people interested in the values NGDOs hold and the agendas they aspire to." "Greater interaction with schools and opportunities for the placement of volunteers within NGDOs would help" (Flowler, 2000).

RESEARCH METHODOLOGY

1. Interview Schedule

The interview schedule was developed according to the three target populations: 1) current Lao NGO senior staff, 2) current expatriate NGO representatives, and 3) former expatriate NGO representatives. Each of the schedules was semi-structured to make it easier to summarize the focusing data. All the informants were resident in Lao PDR and I visited them and conducted face-to-face interviews from June to July in 2002. The questions in the interview schedule and questionnaires consist of both open-ended and closed questions depending on the subject. Using printed formats, I structured each interview session with a standard formula including an introduction, Q&A session, and summary, which took approximately 60 to 90 minutes in total. Basically, the same interview schedule was used for the first and the second informant groups and the simpler version was used for the third informant group (see Appendix 10 and 11).

For detailed questionnaires, I provided questions such as general information of organization (including human resources), perception of localization (definition and synonyms), organizational capacity analysis (with rating from 1 to 5), vision towards localization (opportunities and threats), and NGO leadership (relation with localization), and possibility of local NGOs. I interviewed the current Lao representatives from four international NGOs in Lao PDR. Although they were not structured interviews, indications by each representative contributed to support the background of the research.

2. Target Population and Sampling

As described above, the target population of this study was categorized in three groups. There was a maximum of ten informants in each group.

The first informant group was ten current senior local staff in international NGOs in Lao PDR. Since the subject of localization requires a sense of power relations in each international NGO and knowledge and experience about organizational management, the Lao senior staff were the most important target. For this group, I collected data from all of the ten informants.

The second informants were ten current expatriates working in international NGOs in Lao PDR. They were the key persons with initiatives to plan and implement localization process in collaboration with the headquarters. As planned, I successfully interviewed ten expatriates.

The third informants were people who understood and had experienced the localization process in any developing country. I thought that they could give some important insights and thoughtful comments on this subject. However, as a result, only one informant was interviewed in Lao PDR. It was difficult to collect data for two reasons. The first was that experienced expatriates did not live in Lao PDR and Japan where I conducted face-to-face interviews. For Japanese NGO development workers, the issue of localization seemed like a new study area, as I quickly discovered when I briefly introduced this idea to some Japanese NGO staff. The second reason was that it was time-consuming to find and contact potential informants in the other countries through electronic communication. There was no answer when I sent several messages to potential informants.

For sampling the first and second target groups, I used "Directory of NGOs in Lao PDR 2000", which included a comprehensive listing of International NGOs in Lao

PDR. Since I used to work in Vientiane, Lao PDR, I also contacted NGO staff whom I had met at least once before. I also attempted some 'snow ball' sampling to let my interviewees introduce some other informants.

3. Languages

For conducting interview sessions, I used three languages: English, Lao, and Japanese, according to the target populations. Japanese is my mother tongue and my conversational Lao is almost the same level as my English. I thought that this language flexibility could contribute to bringing more insightful comments from each informant than conducting all sessions in English. I found Lao language more effective for Lao senior staff. I conducted interviews in English or Japanese (with some English explanations) with the current and former expatriates and Lao (with some English explanations) to the current senior Lao staff since they seemed to easily express their experience with the mother tongue. However, my questionnaire forms were written in English as were my notes.

4. Data Summary and Analysis

Collected data was categorized according to a group of questions in the interview schedules. Quantitative data was sorted and displayed with tables to grasp each trend and qualitative data was simplified in the short phrases. In the analysis part, comments were described in a manner of answering my related questions while using models presented in the literature review. For the description, I followed the organizational capacity components by IDRC (Lusthaus, Adrien, Anderson, and Carden, 1999) and partially, referred to 'central versus affiliates' model by Lindenberg and Bryant (2001). Finally, I concluded with the results for my main research question.

FINDINGS

To collect effective interview results, I used the same interview schedule for the Lao senior staff and the expatriates both from international NGOs in Lao PDR. There are six major sections to expect comments to answer my main and detailed research questions; 1) general information about staff and organization, 2) perception of localization, 3) organization capacity analysis, 4) vision of localization, 5) NGO leadership, and 6) local NGOs. I will present the data below according to these six categories.

1. General Information

To select interviewees from international NGOs, I looked through *Directory of NGOs in Lao PDR 2000* (The NGO Directory Committee, 2000) and an ordinary telephone book. I selected some organizations and telephoned to make appointments. My first intention was to make appointments for interview with directors or representatives at the organizations and to let them introduce their senior Lao staff for another interview. Lao staff usually feel comfortable to speak up when their boss approves the interview sessions. Each interview session took approximately 60 to 90 minutes conducted in one of the three languages (English, Lao, or Japanese). In most cases, I gave them an opportunity to read the interview schedule written in English.

Below is the list of interviewees with names of organizations.

The first group and the second group are comparatively major informants because they are actually in the middle of the localization process. Their perceptions are most valuable. On the other hand, I expected the third group, ex-expatriates, to share

Table 4. List of the Interviewees

Expatriate Staff

1. Representative (Action Contre la Faim)
2. Representative (Oxfam Belgium)
3. HR Consultant (World Vision)
4. Representative (Ecoles Sans Frontieres)
5. Representative (CARE Lao PDR)
6. Representative (Save the Children Australia)
7. HRD Coordinator (Norwegian Church Aid)
8. Acting Representative (Japan International Volunteer Center)
9. Representative (ZOA-A Christian Organization for International Refugee Care)
10. Representative (Quaker Service-American Friend Service Committee)
11. Training Advisor (Consortium)
12. Representative (Village Focus International)

Lao Staff

1. Logistician (Action Contre la Faim)
2. Program Manager (CARE Lao PDR)
3. Project Support Coordinator (Save the Children Australia)
4. HRD Officer (Norwegian Church Aid)
5. Program Coordinator (Mennonite Central Committee)
6. Administrator and HRD Officer (ZOA-A Christian Organization for International Refugee Care)
7. Financial Manager (Consortium)
8. Financial Officer (Consortium)
9. Senior Program Coordinator (Quaker Service-American Friend Service Committee)
10. Program Support Officer (Village Focus International)
11. Program Officer (Village Focus International)

Ex-expatriates

1. Former representative (Community Aid Abroad-Oxfam Australia)

Additional Interviewees (Lao representatives of International NGOs)

1. Representative (CIDSE-International Cooperation for Development and Solidarity)
2. Representative (Community Aid Abroad-Oxfam Australia)
3. Representative (Minsai Center)
4. Representative (Association for Sending Picture Books)

their experience about headquarters' policy and the process of capacity building. However, I found it was the most inaccessible target for me because they have been scattered in all over the world. Furthermore, I had to access them by electric communication which has a certain limit in comparison with face-to-face interviews. Since my vital data were something happening in Lao PDR, I decided not to persist in collecting data from the ex-expatriates. Instead of data loss, I obtained some valuable information from the current Lao representatives of four international NGOs. Their perceptions about localization are more interesting and relevant to this study.

2.   Perception of Localization

I provided two questions to understand how much the term "localization" is familiar to the informants. The first question was about basic knowledge for a general meaning of localization. I wrote my definition for localization in the interview form: "in the NGO context, a process of organizational change in management authority from foreign expatriates to local/national staff after a period of capacity building."

All eleven-expatriate staff answered that they knew the meaning of the word 'localization', however, only five Lao staff showed understanding about it. More of the expatriate staff live in the larger NGO society than Lao staff. It is sure that they, as NGO managers, should be familiar with the current NGO development trends. On the other hand, Lao staff has limited to access to the trends because they may not need that kind of information much for their daily work and it may be less accessible if written in English (see Appendix 1).

In the second question, the variety of familiar terms came out from the informants. I put several synonyms for localization and even asked other expressions to describe the condition like localization. This question was interesting because I could know how they use different expressions in their organizations. Seven expatriate staff said, "self-management" was the most familiar word to indicate meaning of localization, then, "nationalization" was the second one (five votes). Four expatriates agreed with "de-centralization" and "indigenization". As other expressions to describe localization, the expatriate informants used terms such as "ownership", "autonomy", "self-determination", "partnership", and "organization change". On the other hand, four Lao staff showed familiarity with both "delegation" and "self-management". As unlisted expression, one Lao staff suggested "hand-over authority" and two said, "transfer". Totally, "self-management" gained eleven votes from both informants. It may indicate that they perceive localization as a process of shifting management authority into Lao people themselves (see Appendix 2).

3. Organization Capacity Analysis

For the third topic, I provided a question to assess current degree of localization with rating 1 (not at all) to 5 (very much) according to five organizational capacity areas; "strategic leadership", "human resources", "financial management", "program management", and "inter-institutional linkages" which were modification of IDRC's categories. Particularly, I omitted "infrastructure" and "organizational process" from the seven areas of organizational capacity by IDRC to simplify the categories while specifying critical areas. "Infrastructure" includes facility and technology management which obviously the Lao staff have been involved with more than expatriates. "Organizational process" is about problem-solving, decision-making, communications, and monitoring and evaluation, which seems to be interdependent with other components.

To look at average scores for each capacity areas, the expatriate shown the following scores on each component": "human resources" (4.3), "program management" (4.2), "financial management" (3.7), "inter-institutional linkages" (3.4), and "strategic leadership" (3). It is interesting to note that the Lao staff showed similar perception to the expatriates such as "human resources" (4.4), "program management" (4), "financial management" (3.8), "inter-institutional linkages" (3.4), and "strategic leadership" able 5.   To what degree has your organization delegated authority to Lao staff ?

Rates Informants & Capacity Areas	1 (Not at all)	2	3	4	5 (Very much)	Average (Points)
Expatriate Staff						
Strategic Leadership		7		3	2	3
Human Resources		1	1	3	7	4.3
Financial Management		2	2	6	2	3.7
Program Management			1	7	4	4.2
Inter-institutional linkages		1	5	6		3.4
Lao Staff						
Strategic Leadership		3	1	2	2	3.4
Human Resources			1	3	4	4.4
Financial Management		1	1	5	1	3.8
Program Management		1		5	2	4
Inter-institutional linkages			5	3		3.4

(3.4). These scores may indicate that "human resource" and "program management" can be identified as the original responsible areas for Lao staff or the areas for
quick delegation to Lao staff. "Strategic leadership" seems the hardest component to
hand over to Lao staff (see Table 5).

4.   Vision of Localization

This section provides more detailed analysis of the process of localization in each organization. The first question is about experience of any discussions about localization among staff. Both expatriate staff and Lao staff said that more than half of each
respondent group had the experience of discussing localization issues in their organization. At the beginning, although some of Lao staff were not familiar with the termi-
nology of localization, they seemed to realize what that meant at this moment. That is
why I could proceed with this question (see Appendix 3).

Table 6.　Ideal Localized Structures According to the Five Alternative Models

Stages / Groups	Separate Independent Organizations & Coalitions	Weak Umbrella Coordinating Mechanisms	Confederations	Federations	Unitary Corporate
	←				→
Current structures of six int'l NGOs		-MSF -Oxfam Int'l	-CARE Int'l -World Vision -Save the Children	-PLAN Int'l	
Future structures of expatriate	-ACF -Oxfam Belgium	-JVC Laos -SCF(Australia)	-CARE Laos -Consortium		
staff in Lao PDR	-ESF -QSL	-ZOA			
Future structures of Lao staff in Lao PDR	-ACF -ZOA -VFI -QSL?	-MCC	-CARE Laos -SCF(Australia) -Consortium -NCA		

Furthermore, I included an open-ended question to get ideas about the goals of local-ization in their organizations. There are several types of vision for localization (see Appendix 4). According to the comments on goals of localization, I would like to cat-egorize the organizations into the five alternative models for association structures by Lindenberg and Bryant (2001). In *Going Global*, Lindenberg and Bryant (2001) assume the current positions where the six organizations have been standing now, however, I have organized the informants' comments into future directions (see Ta-ble 6).

Although the clues to determine which stage each organization would come to are very limited, I think the visions of the expatriate staff present more realistic future structures. They may know what the headquarters would request for their challenge to localization and how other country offices could make a successful localization.

On the other hand, imaginations of the Lao staff may not reach to those levels but they only think about what they would like to be in the future. Accordingly, the comments by the Lao staff tend to be in the separated independent organizations or in the confederations. It means that they show their wishes for independence or maintenance of current structures and the status quo.

The fourth question in the vision of localization was about opportunities and threats against localization (see Appendix 5). As opportunities, expatriate staff were proud of their qualified human resources and stable funding sources. As I showed in the organizational capacity analysis, good human and financial resource management seem to be a strong advantage for proceed towards localization. Therefore, those components were also expressed in threats. For example, there were low English communication skills among Lao staff, not enough qualified staff, difficulties of decision making on HR issues, dishonest activities, and not enough funding sources.

To look at opportunities of Lao staff, it was very interesting that Lao initiatives may bring more effective relationships with service recipients and the Lao government. It was more about inter-institutional linkages according to organizational capacity areas by IDRC. Four informants showed effectiveness in building capacity among local staff. On the other hand, five informants showed a fear of less access to funding sources as one of the many threats and stated concerns about their capacity for organizational management. Finally, it was significant that they also had to express ambivalence about relationships with government such as possible disagreement or pressure for localizing movement. They seem to think of the establishment of Local NGOs as the final destination.

At the end of this section, I asked the informants to prioritize five organizational capacity components of their current performance. In particular, the priority should be rated with numbers from 1 (highest) to 5 (lowest), focusing on successful localization process (see Table 7). Looking at the data of the expatriate staff, five informants put the highest rate on strategic leadership. However, the average was only 2.4 since

Table 7. Priority of Capacity Building Components to Localization

Rates / Informants & Capacity Areas	1 (Highest)	2	3	4	5 (Lowest)	Average	NA
Expatriate Staff							
Strategic Leadership	5		1	1	2	2.4	3
Human Resources	1	3	2	3		2.7	3
Financial Management		4	3	2		2.7	3
Program Management	3	2	2	2		2.3	3
Inter-institutional linkages			1	1	7	4.7	3
Lao Staff							
Strategic Leadership	3	1	1	2		2.3	2
Human Resources	2	2	2	1		2.3	2
Financial Management	2	3	1	1		2.1	2
Program Management		1	3	3		3.3	2
Inter-institutional linkages					7	5	2
Former Expatriate Staff							
Strategic Leadership			1			3	
Human Resources	1					1	
Financial Management					1	5	
Program Management		1				2	
Inter-institutional linkages				1		4	

NA: Not Available-missing data

two other informants gave 5 (lowest) to it. The highest component was program management (2.3) and the lowest one was inter-institutional linkages (4.7).

Lao staff gave the highest priority to financial management (2.1) and the lowest one was inter-institutional linkages (5). It was obvious that inter-institutional linkages were seen to have extremely less priority than any other organizational capacity components for both expatriate staff and Lao staff.

5. NGO leadership

In the fifth section, I attempted to determine how much the NGO leadership would be important to each NGO for successful localization. There are three questions in this section: 1) desirable leadership styles, 2) necessity of leadership for localization, and 3) methods to develop leadership (see Appendix 6 and 7).

There are various kinds of characteristics for NGO leadership (see Table 8). It is possible to identify participatory leaderships both in expatriate and Lao staff. However, it is very hard to identify how those leadership traits related to NGO leadership which Alan Fowler (2000) expressed with the words "creative artists and competent artisans." Most of the informants from the expatriate and Lao staff showed that leadership was necessary to proceed localization. When I asked how to nurture leadership, both informants mentioned every kind of training programs and self-efforts. There is no special remedy for developing NGO leadership in the organizations.

Table 8. What style of leadership do you need for your organization?

Expatriate Staff
- Transparency, independence, professionalism, non-discrimination, and neutrality for fighting to hunger
- Good relation with partners
- Understand staff
- Respect others
- Horizontal approach to staff
- Manager to Office Coordinator
- Consultation skills
- Understand cultural context-Lao people get used to top-down system.
- Using marketing strategy
- Find funds
- Autonomous-not obey to donor's requests but keep own philosophy
- Do as you say-trustful
- Participatory (2)
- Financial management

- Detailed understanding about reality
- Visioning for humanity and human society
- People centered
- Team management skills
- Accountability
- Good balance
- Years of experience and seniority (age)
- Professional background
- Understand jokes
- Good motivation

Lao Staff

- Quality based
- High educational background
- Understand staff, good listener to staff (3)
- Honest person (2)
- Balanced approach between task and people oriented
- Flexibility to cultural, political, and social context
- Understand cultural context
- Good negotiator/mediator among stakeholders
- Open-minded
- Collaborative/participatory (3)
- Not by power
- Team approach (2)
- Sharing authority
- Delegation
- Democratic (people come to talk) (2)
- Quick decision making
- Good following up for decentralized field
- Involving into people
- Research skills
- Give opportunities to others
- Work not for authority or richness but for people' life with peace
- Wide-ranged understanding about people, from bottom to top

6.   Local NGOs

In the last section, I prepared questions to grasp perspectives related to establishing local NGOs. Although all of the informants were from international NGOs, I assumed they definitely had many comments on this issue. As the first question, I asked reasons why local NGOs almost did not exist in Lao PDR (see Appendix 8). There were three main reasons which I could see in the comments of both expatriate and Lao staff: 1) Lao citizens are not motivated enough; 2) international donors do not trust local NGOs yet; and 2) Lao government do not permit local NGO activities. Probably, every reason is believable since they came from their impression and experience of each sector during their daily development activities. However, most informants seemed to mention the Government's negative attitudes towards establishment of local NGOs.

My second question was what actions international NGOs, international donor agencies, and Lao government could take to increase local NGOs (see Appendix 9). There were several interesting actions raised by both the informants:

1)   to give opportunities of exposures about local NGOs for government officials in other countries;

2)   to work in good cooperation with mass-organizations;

3)   to prepare legal framework for local NGOs; to raise this issue at international donor meetings,

4)   to build capacity to understand civil society among government officials;

5)   to invite government officials to NGO meetings.

DATA ANALYSIS

In this section, I examine the above data according to the six related questions（RQ）. To support my main research question which is "what is the most important capacity building component of the process of localizing an International NGO in Lao PDR", I provided the six related questions which mentioned in the Introduction.

RQ 1. What is localization? Which dimensions should be considered in organizational capacity building towards localization?

In the Introduction, I defined localization as a process of organizational change in management authority from foreign expatriates to local/national staff after a period of capacity building in the context of international NGOs. Since all expatriate staff and half of senior Lao staff understood what I would like to convey by this expression, my definition seems to grasp the essence of localization. I assumed that the other half of the Lao staff also understood the meaning of localization but. However, I also figured out that there were different ranges of understanding localization contexts depending on NGO development experience. It means that the most Lao staff tend to talk about it as internal management issues, however, the expatriate staff could think over how it effects the whole picture of the organizations including their headquarters and affiliates. In that sense, I understood that multiple dimensions of localization had to be considered.

Among the synonyms of localization, self-management was comparatively familiar to both informant groups. It might be a desirable condition which people concerned are satisfied with, as a result of localization. However, there are other expressions for localization depending on their own organizational contexts.

To consider organizational capacity dimensions, I introduced seven components of IDRC: "strategic leadership", "human resources", "financial management", "program management", "inter-institutional linkages", "organizational process", and "infrastructure". Then, I applied only the first five components for the interview sessions to make things simpler and focused.   All of the components are very important when you plan organizational change like localization.   However, assessment of the current situation related to localization has shown that "human resources" and "program management" were the most advanced areas in delegating to the Lao staff.   It means that capacity building of both areas is essential to continue implementing development programs in the organizations.   Furthermore, it indicates that other components such as "strategic leadership", "financial management", and "inter-institutional linkages" should comparatively take a long and deliberate process to delegate.   However, it all depends on each organizational policy, culture, management style, and staff capacity.   There might show different ranges of delegation only within one component like human resource management.   For example, decision-making on staff salary must be delegated in a careful manner probably in the latter issue.   The area of "human resources" is considered as faster in delegation according to the results of my research.

RQ 2.   Why do international NGOs localize? Why would they not localize?

To explain the questions, I would like to highlight three major areas which critically impact upon decision-making on promoting or not promoting localization.

First, I would like to raise political reasons in Lao PDR.   The Lao government would like to promote Lao representatives in international NGOs but not in local NGOs.   I explained in the previous section that the Lao government had not yet provided a legal framework for local NGOs.   From my perspective, hopefully, promotion of Lao representatives would facilitate the establishment of local NGOs in future; even if it is a long way in the future.   I think those two issues are interconnected; however, each informant had a different way of looking at the situation. Some of them said they would localize because the government promoted local representatives in their organization. Some told that they would not localize because the government did not approve of local NGOs. When looking at different levels of the localization process, both positive and negative attitudes crop up.

Secondly, organizational or philosophical reasons will influence the attitude towards localization. For example, if an organization has policies or values to foster local initiatives or to create local ownership, localization will be surely promoted. However, there are some organizations which would like to maintain their solid structures and systems or to keep a position not to create any local institutions by their own efforts. The organizational contexts are very diverse.

Thirdly, financial reasons must be explained. From a HR perspective, the cost to attract expatriate staff is very high. I estimate the cost of expatriate salaries at more that ten (sometimes twenty) times that of Lao senior staff. One expatriate staff person provided a positive opinion to localization based on needs of reducing numbers and costs for expatriate salaries. On the other hand, some other expatriate and Lao staff displayed a fear about localization because only local staff might face difficulties accessing funding sources and raising the necessary budgets for development activities.

Aroma Goon, executive director of PRIP Trust, also faced financial difficulty as I described in my literature review. One of my colleagues, Mr. Katsumasa Yagisawa, Asian Regional Director of Shanti Volunteer Association said, "fund-raising can be very difficult if Japanese staff disappear completely. It would be hard for local staff to build trust with Japanese donors directly."

RQ 3.   What is the uniqueness of NGO leadership?

Both the expatriate and Lao staff introduced various NGO leadership styles in the previous section. Some examples could be described like "participatory", "horizontal approach to staff", "people centered" and "not by power", however, that information does not exactly show NGO leadership, which Alan Fowler explained as "creative artists and competent artisans" (2000). I think NGO leadership is too complex to figure out by a few questions and answers. Furthermore, it should be compared with political leadership and business leadership; otherwise, trends of NGO leadership could not be described well.

RQ 4. What are the unique characteristics of international NGOs operating development projects in Lao PDR?

The international NGOs in Lao PDR are seen more as development donor agencies by the government, similarly to UN or bilateral aid agencies, than as facilitators of civil society. The government shows appreciation to the international NGOs only with its economic measurement, not with social values and philosophy. This way of thinking is similar to the attitude which I showed as "political reasons" in RQ.2. They must register their status and get permission to implement development programs according to the NGO decrees (Government of Lao PDR, 1999).

Besides implementing development programs, international NGOs might have some other activities such as advocacy, peace building, and networking to increase civil society. However, the government would not appreciate such kinds of work because they might cause political instabilities. To negotiate with the government or to protest some social problems in public, international NGOs must consider their strategies very well. This is another unique characteristic of international NGOs to in Lao PDR.

RQ 5. What are the lessons from international NGOs, which already have Lao directors?

Although I already briefed the four Lao-directed INGOs in the Introduction, there are some more lessons to be mentioned. There are no common approaches among these four INGOs, however, it is interesting to know that three of them have all female directors.

When I visited the office of CIDSE (Cooperation Internationale pour le Development et la Solidarite), the representative introduced her experience and one unpublished material. That was their discussion paper about localization. CIDSE has field offices in Cambodia, Vietnam, and Lao PDR and each has a local representative after a period of capacity building and delegation. They have discussed their localization plan with European donor agencies in annual retreats. Consultants (who wrote the discussion paper) surveyed three country offices and proposed the nine options to establish independent organizations at each one. The field offices and the European donors take a participatory and culturally sensitive approach to each case of localization. CIDSE prefers to use the term, Autonomy. This case shows a really interesting discussion process from capacity building within each organization to organizational independence (establishment of a local NGO). However, none of them have chosen to change the current name into local ones. The representative explained briefly that changing the organization's name was a big issue.

CAA (Community Aid Abroad, Oxfam Australia) in Lao PDR also has been managed by a Lao representative. CAA sent him to study rural development in Masters Degree course in Thailand. After he received the degree and spent a probation period, CAA welcomed him as a director. He annually goes to headquarters in Australia, negotiate program and budget plans, write several proposals to raise funds, negotiates with the government officials, and supervises human resources in his office. He intimated that Lao government officials feel very comfortable to talk with him because he is a Laotian.

Minsai Center, a Japanese NGO, has been implementing educational programs in Thailand and Lao PDR. Minsai Center has a policy, where headquarters does not send any long term expatriate staff to the field. Therefore, the representative, who was hired as a first Lao staff since a feasibility study period, has managed her office without any expatriates. Her working life is almost the same as CAA's representatives. She complained that a young woman representative was disadvantaged when she negotiated directly with Lao government officials.

ASPB (Association for Sending Picture Books) is also a Japanese NGO, which has been implementing publishing and library promotion projects only in Lao PDR. There are around five staff working with a female Lao representative without any expatriate staff. ASPB used to send a long-term expatriate but shifted into a short term, and stopped sending. Instead, President of ASPB, who is a former Lao exchange student and lives in Japan permanently, often comes to communicate with the Lao office. The representative appears to display strong leadership with her energetic and sincere negotiation skills.

RQ 6. What factors in the current political situation would help or hinder in establishing "indigenous NGOs" in Lao PDR?

There are several factors involved with establishing "indigenous NGOs", however, I would like to briefly mention the political situation. For the "help" first of all, the Lao government would like to have Lao representatives in international NGOs. Although this comment comes from only some informants, I assume it is true. Secondly, the Constitution of Lao PDR defines a people's right to establish associations. This could be a strong point during dialogue in establishing local NGOs.

Thirdly, once the government becomes interested in local NGOs and, perhaps one day in the future, civil society, other socialist countries such as China and Vietnam could help to introduce what they have practiced. Both countries have legally approved local NGOs even though there are some conflicts. Finally, UNDP has attempted to build local models to increase civil society through water supply schemes. It also related this process to the establishment of local institutions. If these models are promoted nation-wide, it will become easier to establish other types of indigenous institutions.

On the other hand, the first reason for "hinder" is that the Lao government has not approved any applications to establish local NGOs. I have heard quite a few people have submitted requests, which have been rejected. Secondly, there is a fear that local NGOs will become political parties against the current government in future. Thirdly, the government thinks mass organizations (Lao Women's Union, Lao Youth Union, Trade Union and the Lao National Patriotic Front for Reconstruction) can take initiatives for grassroots development activities at the national level. This will be one of their strong concepts, which is believed widely from the government officials to ordinary citizens. Finally, NGO decrees have controlled legal status and activities for every international NGOs. Furthermore, the Lao government doesn't approve the establishment of a coordination body for international NGOs. It used to exist but it was dismissed by the government, so now only informal meetings take place monthly without any secretarial service.

CONCLUSION

In this paper, I addressed the research question, "what are the most important capacity building components of the process of localizing an NGO according to NGO staff in Lao PDR". Simplifying the seven organizational capacity models by IDRC, I used five capacity components to conceptualize my interview schedule and to analyze this type of NGO development. My hypothesis was that "strategic leadership" would be the most important capacity area in localization. My thesis was that the effective localization process should be led by local leaders such as Ms. Aroma Goon of PRIP Trust or Mr. Promboon Panitchpakdi of CARE Thailand Foundation. The results of prioritization of the five organizational capacities demonstrate that both expatriate staff and Lao staff gave the highest priority to "strategic leadership". However, the results do not indicate that strategic leadership should be tackled at the beginning of the localization process. When assessing the current organizational capacity for each NGO, both expatriate staff and Lao staff gave "human resources" and "program management" as the most advanced delegated areas. Additionally, fund-raising, which should be in the capacity of the financial resource management, is one of the most difficult areas to localize. In the context of international NGOs, most of the allocated project funds come from the international side. The staff of the headquarters is more responsible for building mutual trust with donors, on the other hand, Lao staff spend considerable time finding alternative fund sources by their own efforts. It is also hard to imagine at present that Lao government, private corporations, foundations, or ordinary citizens will financially support development projects by Lao directed NGOs.

My definition of localization, which is a process of organizational change in management authority from foreign expatriates to local/national staff after a capacity building period in the context of international NGOs, grasps the important essence of localization. However, goals and processes of localization are very diverse depending on each organizational culture and development experience. There are different ranges of understanding between expatriate staff and Lao staff, even among individual staff members. As the most familiar synonym for localization, almost a half of all informants chose "self-management". Against localization as a process, "self-management" can be described as one of the most desirable results.

To understand reasons why or why not international NGOs localize, we must first consider organizational philosophy, government policies regarding NGOs, and funding sources. Organizational willingness can be the core of decision-making towards localization although the organizational contexts are very diverse. If an organization has policies/values to foster local initiatives or to create local ownership, localization will be promoted. If the government's policies and availability of funding sources favorable towards NGOs, the movement to localize is strengthened. This organizational change should happen when some or all of above factors become more critical to organizational stability.

NGO leadership is too complex to describe, however, it seems to be clear that Lao staff need to find alternative leadership characteristics, which they have not experienced in political and/or business firms. "Participatory", "horizontal approach to staff", "people centered", and "not by power" are some examples of the uniqueness of NGO leadership.

The unique situation of international NGOs in Lao PDR is to be seen as development donor agencies, not as facilitators of Lao civil society. The government expects international NGOs to provide enough funds and deliver good development service, not to disturb political stability. Although there are some other features of international NGOs, this situation can be a typical one, which every organization must contend with.

There are some lessons from international NGOs, which already have Lao directors.

CIDSE showed the importance of dialogues between the headquarters and the affiliates to discuss future local initiatives. It is also effective to invite outside consultants to survey each country context and to provide opportunities to share what they face among three affiliates. CAA experienced a successful leadership training process. The headquarters provided an opportunity of higher education (masters degree) to the potential local leader and promoted him as director. Since he studied rural development at a nearby university, trust building with other local staff was smoothly done. A policy of Minsai Center, where the headquarters does not send any long-term expatriate staff to the field, is also a key to successful localization. The organization can be quickly localized with staff sent by the headquarters and then start working in its own capacity. A choice of Lao-directed international NGO from birth is an effective organizational strategy. ASPB reveals a communicative top management system between the President and the field director. Since both are Lao women and the President visits the field office very often, their language barrier and conflict between the headquarters and the affiliate are almost nonexistent.

Considering the current Lao political situation, there are both opportunities for and threats to establishing "indigenous NGOs". The opportunities include: 1) a preference for Lao-directed international NGOs; 2) the definition of the people's right to establish associations in the Constitution, 3) the existence of local NGOs in other socialist countries, and 4) trials to increase civil society organizations by UNDP. The threats tend to be 1) the tendency to reject the applications of local NGOs, 2) fear that NGOs will become anti-government parties, 3) the existence of mass organizations to implement development projects, and 4) strict NGO decrees. It is difficult to figure out which factor is a stronger influence on establishing "indigenous NGOs". However, it is possible that local NGOs might appear slowly in Lao civil society.

Finally, I conclude that fostering strategic leadership within international NGOs is the most important factor of capacity development related to the issue of localization. Since NGO leadership differs from political and/or business forms, there is no place to learn but within International NGOs. The four approaches to fostering local initiatives among international NGOs can contribute to other organizations. Then, leaders who are developed within international NGOs, would also be potential leaders for future local NGOs. It is one of the most effective ways to enlarge civil society in Lao PDR.

RECOMMENDATIONS

I would like to contribute my research to international NGOs in Lao PDR, Japanese NGOs, and my own organization. For the international NGOs in Lao PDR, which were also my informants, this paper might establish one way in which they can choose to become Lao-directed international NGOs or local NGOs. Many ideas, steps, and examples are given in this paper. A good start would be the inclusion of a timetable for localization as part of each organization's broader strategic plan.

As a member of a Japanese NGO operating in Lao PDR, I would like to introduce the concept of localization to other Japanese NGOs, which have been operating development projects overseas while setting up field offices. From my understanding, there are very few Japanese NGO staff familiar with the idea of localization. They are very enthusiastic about implementing projects together with the local staff, but they have not started to plan for the future by building institutional capacity in the field. I expect to learn some interesting localization practices from other Japanese NGOs. I would nonetheless still introduce the concepts and lessons discovered when researching this paper because many of the Japanese NGOs have already promoted the localization process without any solid plan and goal for its achievement in practice.

Finally, my organization will soon be ready to apply a conceptual framework of localization in its organizational strategic plan. Localization is a hot issue both in the field offices and in the headquarters. In making a basic plan for our future organizational structures and in practicing discussion at all levels, I am sure that this paper will contribute to our organization and to development and governance activities in general.

BIBLIOGRAPHY

Allison, M., and Kaye, Jude. *Strategic Planning for Nonprofit Organizations: A Practical Guide and Workbook.* John Wiley & Sons, 1999.

Asian Development Bank. *A Study of NGOs: Lao People's Democratic Republic,* 1999.

Lusthaus, Charles., Adrien, Marie-Helene., Anderson, Gary., and Carden, Fred. *Enhancing Organizational Performance: A Toolbox for Self-Assessment.* International Development Research Centre,1999.

Church World Service Cambodia. *Program Plan 2001-2003.* Unpublished document, 2001.

Fowler, Alan. *The Virtuous Spiral: A Guide to Sustainability for Non-Governmental Organizations in International Development.* Eathscan Publications Ltd, 2000.

Government of Lao PDR. *Decree of the Prime Minister on the Administration of Non-Governmental Organizations (NGOs) in the Lao People's Democratic Republic.* 1998 & *Guidelines for the Implementation of the Decree of the Prime Minister on the Administration of Non-Governmental Organizations (NGOs) in the Lao People's Democratic Republic.* 1999.

Korten, David.C. *Getting to the 21st Century: Voluntary Action and the Global Agenda.* Kumarian Press, Inc,1989.

Leermakers, Mieke. *INGOs in Transition: Strategies applies towards local leadership in Nepal. Unpublished research document,* 2002.

Levinger, Beryl., and Bloom, Evan. *Discussion –Oriented Organizational Self-Assessment (DOSA).* Website: http://www.edc.org/GLG/CapDev/dosafile/capareas.htm, 1997.

Lindenberg, Marc., and Bryant, Coralie. *Going Global: Transforming Relief and Development NGOs.* Kumarian Press, Inc, 2001.

Newman, W.Lawrence. *Social Research Methods: Quantitative and Qualitative Approaches.* A Viacom Company, 1991.

Parameshwar, Sangeeta. *On Becoming a Local NGO: PRIP's Metamorphosis-An Interview with Aroma Goon, Executive Director of PRIP Trust.* Website: http://connection.cwru. edu/ai/gem/aromafinal.doc,

Payton, David. *Transforming an International Development Project into a Local NGO.* SIT Occasional Papers Series, Issue Number 2, Spring 2001: World Learning, 2001.

Peberdy, Max., and Pearson, Jenny. *CIDSE: Exploratory Study of the Options for the Future of the CLV Programs: Report prepared for the Cambodia, Laos and Vietnam Coordinating Committee Meeting, June 2002.* Unpublished document, 2002.

Smille, Ian., and Hailey, John. *Managing for Change: Leadership Strategy and Management in Asian NGOs.* Agakhan Foundation Canada: Earthscan Publications Ltd, 2001.

Tarr, Amy. *Managing Change or Running to Catch Up?: CARE USA and its Mission in Thailand.* Kennedy School of Government Case Program C18-95-1281.0: Harvard University, 1995.

The NGO Directory Committee. *Directory of NGOs in Lao PDR 2000., 2000.*

UNDP CSOPP Resource Center. *Laos: Building Local Models for a National Civil Society., 2000.*

Yukl, Gary. *Leadership in Organizations: Fourth Edition.* Prentice-Hall, Inc, 1998.

APPENDICES

Appendix 1.   Have you heard about localization?

Responses / Informants	Expatriate Staff	Lao Staff	Former Expatriate Staff	Lao Representatives	Total
Yes	11	5	1	2	19
No		3		1	4

Appendix 2.   Which terms are more familiar to describe meaning of localization?

Synonyms / Informants	Expatriate Staff	Lao Staff	Former Expatriate Staff	Lao Representatives	Total
From Choices					
De-centralization	4	3			7
Evolution	3	1			4
Devolution	2				2
Delegation	3	4			7
Indigenization	4				4
Self-management	7	4			11
Nationalization	5	2			7
Others					
Ownership	1	1	1		3
Autonomy	1				1
Self-determination	1	1			2
Partnership	1				1
Organizational change	1				1
Hand-over authority		1			1
Transfer		2			2

Appendix 3.   Have you ever discussed about localization in your organization?

Responses / Informants	Expatriate Staff	Lao Staff	Former Expatriate Staff	Lao Representatives	Total
Yes	8	5	1		14
No	3	3	0		6

Appendix 4.　Goals of Localization

Expatriate Staff

ACF: Localization is a reason "why we are here". If ACF sees no humanitarian issues in Lao PDR, there is no involvement by ACF. Our style is to "phase-out" as soon as possible problematic situation is finished and competency is transferred. It is good to see local NGOs or government partners to continue development programs in Laos. It is fine with no name of ACF.

Oxfam Belgium: The goal will be the day when Oxfam Belgium does not have to be a coordinating institution. It means that Oxfam Belgium (any Oxfam families) are not in position to create any development coordinating institution. Not for local NGOs but locally managed.

World Vision: The goal is to create ownership among local staff. Even Lao representative come to manage the office, World Vision keeps a membership without changing the name. Comparing to that stage, the Lao office is still like a baby. Representative of World Vision Philippines is a Filipinos.

ESF: Reducing a number of expatriates is the first step. Then, delegate responsibilities of expatriates to potential local senior staff as much as possible. Headquarters will take a role as an advisory and funding agency. It is free to think about a new name and logo for the newly created local ESF.

CARE: Although we start with CARE and then local staff become more responsible, CARE is still CARE. It is not a NGO but a development business agency. Ownership should be developed in the office.

JVC: Management by Lao manager will be preferable. Ability of fund-raising is the most critical issue to identify it "localized". Japanese staff can focus more about advocacy and exchange programs than field activities.

SCF: It is favorable that there are no expatriates and Lao staffs take over all positions including the representative. Indeed, hiring expatriates is very expensive. We have to think about a cost-effective manner. Also, it may be true that Lao staff and Lao governmental counterparts are not comfortable to have a lot of expatriates these days.

QSL: To reach to the more localized organization, local staff must develop fund raising and report writing (particularly in English) skills. A biggest part of the fund-raising skill is proposal writing. To proceed fund raising successfully, Lao workers have to build up capacity on networking in both the domestic and the international contexts. Roles of expatriates shift to more advisory ones.

<u>ZOA</u>: Office of Lao PDR is expected to become an affiliate. Changing power relations between expatriates and local staff, we expect to have national representative with expatriate advisor in near future. Then, discussion to become a local NGO will come up.

<u>Consortium</u>: To shift Lao project manager to Office manager, we need to take a lot of training stages. Consortium is not thinking seriously about that kind of process.

<u>GAPE</u>: No descriptions

Lao staff

<u>ACF</u>: In future, Lao should be a representative of ACF. Then, the office can change the name to become a local NGO. However, it should be a translation of ACF. In the organization, we use the Lao language as a common one.

<u>CARE</u>: CARE is not so trustful to local staff although the Lao government asks Lao staff to take more responsibility. Fund raising is the hardest task for Lao staff to take over. Lao staff is motivated to become Management Representative.

<u>SCA</u>: It is difficult to raise fund in Lao PDR. So, it is better to keep an alliance of Save the Children Australia. In Lao culture, people believe that it is stable to go with a famous organization.

<u>MCC</u>: MCC has been promoting local movement at community level. Five years from now, it is expected that Lao national become a representative.

<u>ZOA</u>: Lao national staff should be coming up to a country manager, which is a current expatriate position. It is favorable if we could choose a Lao name for our organization. In the same manner, project office should be localized. Governmental administration units could be potential development organizations. Capacity building is necessary to district officers in district development committees.

<u>Consortium</u>: The obvious indicator is that Lao country director will represent Consortium Lao PDR. However, fund-raising may have to depend on expatriates for a while. We wish the team like a family even the director change into a Lao national.

<u>GAPE</u>: A local NGO is our final destination. Maybe an expatriate could support as a volunteer but a director/manager. Name is unknown.

<u>QSL</u>: No description

<u>NCA</u>: In our regional strategic plan (three years), it is called Nationalization. That is our goal of localization.

Appendix 5.   Opportunities and Threats against Localization

Expatriate Staff

Opportunities:

- Existing committed staff
- Good people-qualified staff
- Localized NGOs have better status than International NGOs
- Aware of management budget
- Be able to use own languages
- Create confident staff capacity
- Ability to keep information network
- Optional status for ACF to come back in future

Threats:

- Low communication skill in English
- How to deal conflicts with government
- A pool of people is limited
- Staff is moving to other organizations
- Less time management skills
- No time for long term training
- Take time for trust making with others
- No funding sources
- Different decision making for HR issues
- No Funding source such as Child Sponsorship of World Vision
- Heavier responsibility than before
- Dishonest activities will happen
- A lot of pressure

Lao Staff

Opportunities:

- Lao initiative
- Lao helps Lao-Lao understand Lao culture (2)
- Be able to learn international methods

- Be able to build capacity for local staff effectively (4)
- Reduce expenditure for expatriates (2)
- Trust with recipients is sustainable
- More direct responsibility on social needs
- Lao become as a working language and make all communication smooth
- Maybe Lao start supporting fund by themselves
- Easier to communicate with the government
- A variety of NGOs will emerge in the Lao society
- Leadership in Int'l NGO encourages to establish local NGOs in future

Threats:

- Less capacity for sustainability
- Too much flexibility on organizational capacity
- Less access to funding sources (5)
- Less management experiences
- No experience of democracy and justice
- Team work is still under developed
- Lao government face difficulty to control NGOs
- Less experience to keep international standard in working systems
- No approval by the government (2)
- Hard to find a right individual as a director
- The government makes limitation to local NGOs
- Struggle with political pressure by Government
- Meet to original need and reality of villagers
- Lao staff can design organizational structure

Appendix 6.   The leadership is critical for promoting localization?

Responses \ Informants	Expatriate Staff	Lao Staff	Former Expatriate Staff	Lao Representatives	Total
Yes	6	7			13
No	2				2

Appendix 7.   How would you like to nurture the NGO leadership within your organization?

Expatriate Staff
- Send them to higher education
- "Learning matrix" for every staff (duration: three years)
- Opportunities to study abroad (2)
- English language
- Participate international workshops
- Through on the job training
- Formal training
- Not by others but by themselves, trial and error by themselves
- Through international exchange in community development
- On the job training (2)
- Offsite training
- Through all possible self-training (2)
- Coaching after delegation, then assessment
- Mentoring and coaching
- Giving opportunities to do own work
- Mentoring— give suggestions and let them make decisions
- Planed human resource training (3-5 year)

Lao Staff
- Skill up for financial management
- Leadership training inside/outside countries
- On-site training
- Technical training
- Managerial training
- Cross visits
- As a process: preparation-design capacity building-OJT-off/onsite training- study visit to other NGOs-following up and assessment
- Study abroad-to gain diversified values
- Promotion
- Prepare for scholarship
- Review Job performance system from administration to programs
- Coaching by advisors (2)
- Regional workshop: meet local staff from other countries every two year
- Case study on leadership
- Annual capacity building workshop
- Self-study
- Training program
- On the Job Training (2)
- Delegation
- Mentoring
- Retreat workshop

Appendix 8. What are the main reasons why there are almost no Local NGOs in Lao PDR?

Expatriate Staff

- Political situation—to keep single party system (3)
- Oxfam expect to be created Lao NGOs, but in many countries, it comes from outside with money. NGO is professional organization and those organizations are coming from side of people (bottom).
- Capacity is not ready yet. Not much greater needs. NGO should come from internal motivation. Local NGOs for what?
- Socialist government wants mass organizations to take initiatives on development projects, not INGOs or local NGOs. (2) Lao Women's Union, Youth Union, and Labor Union could reach to the bottom. Why local NGOs?
- To maintain "peace" and security
- Threat for anti-government movement — afraid for arrested.
- Government feels hard to control local NGOs.
- Government system does not allow setting up local NGOs. They are afraid of NGOs. Local NGOs may be comparatively poor. (2)

Lao Staff

- Government does not yet give opportunities to establish it.
- Government is afraid of being against a single party system.
- Lao government thinks Lao people could support each other without NGOs.
- Lao government does not approve it yet. (3)
- People are also afraid of asking to establish local NGOs.
- Individuals in the Lao society, even governmental officials, do not understand a term of NGOs
- In Asia, there is a difficulty to find funding sources. International donors do not trust local NGOs for funding.

Appendix 9. To increase Local NGOs, what actions should international NGOs, international donor agencies and Lao government take?

Expatriate Staff

- Although regime is not fostering local NGOs, it is better to show one example of local NGOs to government.
- Many INGOs would like to support local NGOs. International agencies should push the government. It is good to invite Lao government officers to study tour to see local NGOs in other countries.
- Think seriously how much time, energy, money you spend to build capacity on local staff. Many of them will just leave.
- If mass organizations take initiatives on development works, local NGOs could be strengthened.
- International NGOs put pressure on Lao government to become more open towards local NGOs.
- Government should prepare legal policy support.
- Government deliberates (consider carefully) over local NGOs. So, we have to wait for the time. INGOs should focus on capacity building. Donor agencies could suggest to Lao government for strengthening local NGOs.
- This is not Oxfam's agenda. There are misunderstanding about International NGOs.
- Embassies can encourage Lao government to attention to local society at International donor meetings.

Lao Staff

- International donor agencies should give opportunities and sources to set up local NGOs.
- They should also negotiate with Lao government for a legal status as a local NGO.
- Government should build their capacity to understand a civil society and NGOs.
- Lao government should approve local NGOs.
- Lao government should understand NGOs first— Lao government is OK with village development organizations but not with local NGOs.
- Government is favorable with localized INGOs, so the staff in the localized INGOs will choose local NGOs in future. One day, the government will approve local NGOs.
- Leadership training and advisory support by INGOs will lead to establish local NGOs. Lao staff could manage in financial issues.
- Informal NGO meetings should invite Lao government officials to facilitate understanding NGOs among the authority.
- Donor agencies and INGOs will negotiate to put a pressure on Lao government to approve local NGOs.

Appendix 10.   Interview Schedule (1)

Target respondents: [   ] Laotian Senior staff of INGOs (10 informants)
                           [   ] Expatriates of INGOs (10 informants)

Part I: General Information

1-1. Name of the organization:

1-2. Interviewee:

1-3. Title:

1-4. Place:

1-5. Date:

1-6. Current major development programs in the organization:

1)

2)

3)

4)

5)

1-7. Brief history of your development working experience (including changing responsibilities):

⟨Organization name⟩   ⟨responsibilities⟩   ⟨years of service⟩

1)

2)

3)

4)

1-8. How many expatriates do work at your field office? What are their titles /responsibilities?

⟨Titles/Responsibilities⟩   ⟨Number⟩

1)

2)

3)

4)

5)

1-9. How many Laotian staffs do work at your field office? What are their titles/responsibilities?

⟨Titles/Responsibilities⟩   ⟨Number⟩

1)

2)

3)

4)

5)

6)

7)

8)

9)

10)

Part II: Perception of localization

2-1. Have you heard a word, *localization* in the NGO context, which refers "a process of organizational change in management authority from foreign expatriates to local/national staff after a period of capacity building"? Yes / No

2-2. Which terms are more familiar to you to describe above meaning of *localization*?
[   ] De-centralization [   ] Evolution [   ] Devolution [   ] Delegation
[   ] Indigenization [   ] Self-management [   ] Nationalization
[   ] Others
specifically:
NB: Interviewer asks for a permission to use *localization* for convenience in following questions.

Part III: Organizational Capacity Analysis

In following organizational capacity components, to what degree do you think your organization has delegated its authority to Laotian staff? In this case, please consider your field office as an organization.

3-1. Strategic leadership
(Organizational leadership, strategic planning, governance, structure, and niche management)
   1 (not at all)   2   3   4   5 (very much)
Comments on strategic leadership issues:

3-2. Human resource management
(Planning, staffing, developing, appraising and rewarding, and maintaining effective human-resource relations)
   1 (not at all)   2   3   4   5 (very much)
Comments on human resource issues:

3-3. Financial management
(Financial planning, fundraising, financial accountability, and financial statements and systems)
   1 (not at all)   2   3   4   5 (very much)
Comments on financial management issues:

3-4. Program management
(Planning, implementation, and monitoring/evaluation of programs/projects)
   1 (not at all)   2   3   4   5 (very much)
Comments on program process management issues:

3-5. Inter-institutional linkages
(Planning, implementing, and monitoring networks and partnerships with other NGOs, donors, governmental counterparts, headquarters)
   1 (not at all)   2   3   4   5 (very much)
Comments on inter-institutional linkage issues:

Part IV: Vision of Localization

4-1. Have you ever discussed about for localization in your organization?

Yes   / No   If yes, specifically:

4-2. What is your goal of localization? What kind of changes would you identify in your localized organization? Please describe it briefly. (For example, number of expatriates and Lao staff, responsibilities, legal registrations, organization's name, fund sources, office locations, communication systems, common languages, and vision/mission etc.)

4-3. What do you think of opportunities and threats against the localization?

   Opportunities: Threats:

4-4. Among the five areas of organizational capacity above described, what priority do you put on each in terms of importance to contribute to the successful localization? Please put numbers 1 (highest priority) to 5 (lowest priority).

[   ] Strategic leadership   Comments: [   ] Human resources
[   ] Financial management
[   ] Program management
[   ] Inter-institutional linkages

Part V: NGO Leadership

5-1. What style of leadership do you need for your organization? Please introduce your models of leadership if you have.

5-2. Do you think the NGO leadership is critical for promoting localization? Yes / No

5-3. How would you like to nurture the NGO leadership within your organization?

Part VI: Local NGOs

6-1. What do you think of the main reason why there are almost no Local NGOs in Laos?

6-2. To increase Local NGOs in Laos, what actions should International NGOs take? What about international donor agencies and Lao government?

                                        Thank you very much for your cooperation.

Appendix 11. Interview Schedule (2)

Target respondents: [   ] Former Expatriates of INGOs (10 informants)

Part I: General Information

1-1. Name of the current organization:

1-2. Interviewee:

1-3. Title:

1-4. Place:

1-5. Date:

1-6. Brief history of your development working experience (including changing responsibilities):
         〈Organization name〉   〈responsibilities〉   〈years of service〉

1)

2)

3)

4)

Part II: Experience of Localization

2-1. Have you used a word, localization in the NGO context, which refers "a process of organizational change in management authority from foreign expatriates to local/national staff after a period of capacity building"?   Yes / No

2-2. How have you discussed, planned, or implemented the localization in your previous NGOs (including discussions with your head office)？ Please describe your experience with localization briefly.

2-3. What was the goal of localization? What kind of changes did you identify in your localized organization? For example, changes in — number of expatriates and Lao staff, responsibilities, legal registrations, organization's name, fund sources, office locations, communication systems, common languages, and vision/mission etc.

2-4. Which terms can describe similar approaches /processes to localization?
[   ] De-centralization   [   ] Evolution   [   ] Devolution   [   ] Delegation
[   ] Indigenization   [   ] Self-management   [   ] Nationalization
[   ] Others
specifically:

Part III: Organizational Capacity for Localization

3-1. Among the following organizational capacity components, in general, what priority would you prefer to strengthen organizational capacity towards a successful localization? Please put numbers 1 (first) to 5 (last) if you could describe it as a step-by-step approach.

[   ] Program management
(Planning, implementation, and monitoring/evaluation of programs/projects)

[   ] Financial management
(Financial planning, fundraising, financial accountability, and financial statements and systems)

[   ] Strategic leadership
(Organizational leadership, strategic planning, governance, structure, and niche management)

[   ] Inter-institutional linkages
(Planning, implementing, and monitoring networks and partnerships with other NGOs, donors, governmental counterparts, headquarters)

[   ] Human resource management
(Planning, staffing, developing, appraising and rewarding, and maintaining effective human-resource relations)

Part IV: NGO Leadership

4-1. What style of leadership do you think important for NGOs? Please suggest some unique traits/ characteristics of the NGO leadership.

4-2. What staff development methods do you think effective to nurture the NGO leadership? For example, off-site training workshops, on the job training, mentoring, coaching, and self-learning, etc.

4-3. Do you think the NGO Leadership capacity is critical for localization process? Yes / No
Why do you think so?

Thank you very much for your cooperation.

Appendix 12.　Pictures in Lao PDR

Small fishing boats on the Mekong river in the evening. The other side is Thailand.
©Shanti Voluntear Association

A view of World Heritage Town, Luang Prabang, Northern Laos.
©Takehiro Ono

Lao dishes made with a lot of herb and vegetable. They go well with steamed sticky rice.
©Takehiro Ono

Fresh seasonal vegetable and fruits in morning street market.
©Takehiro Ono

Lao traditional hand woven skits, Sinh. It's a important formal garment for women.

©Takehiro Ono

An old wooden school building made by villagers. It's time for renewal.

©Shanti Voluntear Association

Children are always eager to learn under any circumstance.
©Shanti Voluntear Association

Children enjoy playing football in front of a new school building.
©Shanti Voluntear Association

76

Evaluation workshop with local education officers, teachers, and NGO staff.
©Shanti Voluntear Association

Training workshop making educational printed materials with a simple roneo
printing machine.   ©Shanti Voluntear Association

Reading promoting programs with a bookmobile at a primary school.
©Shanti Voluntear Association

Children enjoy reading at a new school library space. Surely need more books.
©Shanti Voluntear Association

著者略歴

小 野　豪 大（おの　たけひろ）

1963 年　北海道美唄市生まれ
2004 年　米国 SIT（School for International Training，SIT 大学院大学）国際異文化間マネジメント修士課程修了
ジモノ工房プロジェクト共同代表，北海道教育大学非常勤講師
tono63110@gmail.com

Localizing NGO Leadership in Lao Civil Society

2021 年 9 月 30 日　第 1 刷発行　　　　　　　　　　・検印省略

　　　　　　　　　　　　　　　著　者　小 野 豪 大

　　　　　　　　　　　　　　　発行者　木 村 慎 也

・定価はカバーに表示　　　　　　　印刷　中央印刷／製本　川島製本

発行所　株式会社 北 樹 出 版

〒153　東京都目黒区中目黒 1-2-6　電話（03）3715-1525（代表）